TALES OF TRAVEL AND TRUST

TALES OF
TRAVEL AND
TRUST

OUR CELTIC HERITAGE

JOHANNA O'MAHONY WALTERS

VERITAS

First published 1999 by
Veritas Publications
7/8 Lower Abbey Street
Dublin 1

Copyright © Johanna O'Mahony Walters 1999

ISBN 1 85390 459 7

Designed by Bill Bolger
Illustrations by Jeanette Dunne
Printed in the Republic of Ireland by Betaprint Ltd, Dublin

For David and Neil with love.

CONTENTS

Acknowledgements

My thanks to my friends Jean, Eleanor, Roger and the late Brian Kelly (who was at the conception but sadly not at the birth of this book) for their love and support. Thanks to my friends Sister Mary and Sister Phil who provided the instructions for the making of the Brigid's Cross.

Timeline

The Iron Age	800 BC
Celts	Birth of Christ
Celts	100 AD
Roman British Period	400 AD
	432 AD Patrick
	452 AD Brigid
	480 AD Tydfil
	486 AD Ita
	490 AD Brendan
	500 AD Non
	510 AD Illtyd
	520 AD David
	521 AD Columcille
	550 AD Brynach
	600 AD Gobnait
	640 AD Winefride
Post–modern period	1999 AD

These are approximate dates. Nobody knows for certain when these saints were born or when they died. It was a very long time ago.

INTRODUCTION

As you can see from the timeline, the people you will read about in this book lived a long time ago. Even so, they were real people who loved and laughed and played and sang, just like you and me. We now call them 'saints', people who were kind and good and who lived in peace and harmony with their fellow beings. I'm sure you can think of people like that who live quite close to you. Close your eyes and 'see' some person who is kind and helpful, who perhaps loves animals, is kind to old and sick people, someone who smiles a lot – a happy person with whom you enjoy spending time. I'm sure you've heard grown-ups refer to these people as 'saints' or, perhaps, 'angels'.

The Celtic saints that we will read about all had one thing in common – they all loved nature. They were at home in the woods, in the mountains, beside the sea; they had a special love for animals and birds and very often kept them as pets and talked to them, rather like Francis of Assisi.

The stories in this book are truths but not necessarily facts. The people lived so long ago – before people knew how to write – that all the stories have come down by word of mouth, and you know what happens when you play 'Chinese whispers' – yes, the story changes. So let's call these stories 'legends' - they tell about real people, which gives us some insight into the kind of people they were.

I hope you enjoy reading about these people who liked all the things that you like. Take away the television, telephone, electricity, supermarkets, etc. and think about what you like doing – playing with a friend, singing, climbing trees, swimming in the sea or river (the water was clean then!), smelling flowers, listening to the birds singing – all those things which really make us feel alive.

Now I hope you will enjoy these tales of people who lived in Wales and Ireland in the fourth and fifth centuries. Perhaps one day you too will feel your connectedness to the Creator of such beauty.

PATRICK

Patrick was a blue-eyed, happy young boy living on the west coast of Wales. His dad was a Roman officer. Patrick spent a lot of his time wandering and exploring along the seashore with his friends, whose dads were also in the Roman army.

Irish pirates were constantly roaming along the coast looking for slaves and valuable Roman artefacts to take back to Ireland. One day while Patrick was collecting shells along the beach with two of his friends, they were set upon by a group of very fierce-looking pirates. His friends managed to escape but Patrick stumbled and fell over a rock. He was caught by one of the pirates who dragged him onto his boat and set sail for Ireland. He was terrified of these fierce angry-looking men.

When they reached Ireland, Patrick was sold as a slave to an Irish chieftain called Milchu, who sent him to look after sheep on a high mountain in County Antrim called Slieve Mish. It was a very lonely life for a young boy. He was often cold and hungry and he missed his home and family in Wales. He spent a lot of his time praying and singing, and at night-time he made friends with the stars. He became very familiar with the stars and gave them names. During the day the birds sang to him and flew onto his shoulders and onto his hands.

One cold, starry night, an angel appeared to Patrick. He was frightened at first because he had never met an angel before, but the angel was so beautiful and so friendly that his fear soon vanished. The angel told him to make his way to the coast where a ship would be waiting to take him home. He travelled along the route the angel had described to him. He travelled about two hundred miles in all, and eventually found the ship waiting for him in the harbour. He went on board and was safely taken home to his family.

Years later, he went to France to study because he wanted to become a priest. One night he heard the voices of the Irish children calling him in a dream, begging him to come back to them and tell them all about Jesus. He did not really want to return to Ireland, but he knew this is what God wanted of him, so when he became a priest he returned to Ireland and taught the Irish people about Jesus.

He is still much loved in Ireland. He is Ireland's patron saint and Irish people all over the world celebrate his feastday on 17 March. That day is a national holiday in Ireland.

Irish Emblems

'There's a dear little plant that grows in our Isle
'Twas St Patrick himself sure that set it
It grows through the woods and bog and the mireland
And they call it the dear little shamrock of Ireland.'

The shamrock is a tiny plant with three leaves on one stem. Patrick is said to have used this plant to explain the doctrine of the Trinity (three persons in one God) to the Irish people. Irish people wear this plant with pride on St Patrick's Day and send it to their relatives all over the world, so that they too may be part of the celebration of Irishness. The shamrock grows wild in Ireland, but a cultivated variety is grown elsewhere.

Can you find some?
How does it differ from clover?
Can you compose your own poem/song in praise of this tiny but very significant plant?
Perhaps you could decorate it nicely and send it as a St Patrick's Day gift to a relative living in another country.

'The harp that once through Tara's hills
The soul of music shed...'

The harp is the national musical instrument
of both Wales and Ireland.
It makes very beautiful music.
Can you find some harp music?
If not, try the library.
Sit quietly with your eyes closed and listen to this harp music. Afterwards, paint or draw or make a collage of what you 'see' as you listen. Put your artwork on your bedroom wall to remind you of this beautiful music which is in your soul.

BRIGID

Brigid is a really important Irish saint, almost as important as Patrick. She was a beautiful girl, tall and elegant. Her mother was a slave and her father a powerful Irish chieftain who lived in a castle in Kildare. Brigid was accustomed to having whatever she wanted.

Many of the young Irish princes wanted this vivacious and talented girl as a wife, but she did not want any of them – she had made up her mind to become a nun. Her family was very unhappy about her decision and promised her rare and precious jewels if she would change her mind. But she was a determined young girl and said, 'This is what God wants of me, so it is what I must do. I really do not wish to offend any of you, so do try to understand why I am doing this.'

So off she went to a nearby hillside and founded a convent. Some more young girls soon joined her and before long it was a thriving community. They were often seen visiting the poor and the sick, teaching young people and looking after animals and birds. They lived simple, prayerful lives, eating only the vegetables they grew.

Brigid was a good nurse, familiar with the healing properties of the herbs and plants which grew locally. Many miracles were performed through her. Once when she was seeking land for her community, she asked the King of Leinster for as much land as her cloak would cover. He granted her request, thinking that such a small amount of land was of no use to him. When Brigid put her cloak down on the ground, the cloak spread out over most of the curragh – now famous for horse-racing.

Once while Brigid was nursing an old chieftain who was dying, she started plaiting rushes off the floor into a cross. The chieftain asked,

'What are you making?' She explained that she was making a cross. He then asked her what the significance of the cross was, and she told him the story of Jesus from his birth in a stable to his death on the cross. He was so moved by the story that he asked to be baptised before he died. It is still customary on 1 February – the Feast of Brigid – to plait Brigid's crosses in the hope that they will protect the household in the year ahead.

How to Make a Brigid's Cross

Materials:
- Rushes (fresh ones are ready to use, dry ones need to be soaked in warm water.) It is useful to have several rushes bent in half before you start as you will need both hands until the cross is secure.
- Scissors
- Elastic bands

1. Take a bunch of rushes and trim both ends to the same length.
2. Take one rush and hold it horizontally.
3. Bend a second rush in half, and place it in the centre of the first to make a T-shape.
4. Now bend a third rush in half, over and under the second and slide it along the first.
5. Bend a fourth rush in half, over and under the third and the first. Repeat steps 4 and 5, turning the cross a quarter turn to the right each time, building up the cross as you go.
6. When the four arms are roughly the same thickness, tie securely near the end of each arm and trim the ends to the same length.

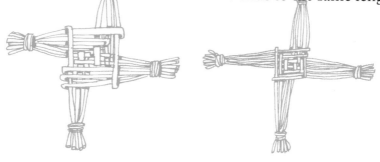

TYDFIL

Little is known about this young girl who belonged to a very large family. Her father was called Brychan. He is said to have come across from Ireland and lived with his wife and children in the Brecknockshire area in mid-Wales. Being a large family, Tydfil and her brothers and sisters had a lot of fun, wandering in the Beacons, swimming in the rivers and playing among the heather and the gorse. Tydfil had a great love of the flowers and plants that grew in that area. She was a good artist and spent many hours drawing these beautiful flowers. She was also familiar with the healing properties of herbs, and people came to her for herbal remedies for their various ailments.

Her older brothers and sisters were leaving home to become nuns or monks and she began to think about her own future. She had always prayed as a child, but she loved the outdoor life and was not so sure about spending her days in a convent. She did want to serve God and to heal people and animals.

She went to live a solitary life in what is today known as Merthyr Tydfil. There she prayed, gathered herbs from the surrounding countryside and made up medicines for the local people. She became well-known and loved in the area because she had saved the lives of so many people with her wonderful cures.

One day while she was going on a visit to her father Brychan, who was now very old and quite ill, she was attacked by robbers and killed. Her family was very angry and upset, and her brothers got an army together and chased the robbers out of the area.

The town Merthyr Tydfil – Martyr of Tydfil – is named after her. There are also two islands just off the Lleyn peninsula named after her, and a small chapel dedicated to her on one of the islands. Her feastday is kept on 23 August.

Earth

Look in your garden.
How many different coloured flowers can you see?
Do you know the names of these flowers?
Do the prettiest flowers have the nicest smells?
Look very closely at a flower; use a magnifier if you wish.
Can you name the different parts?
Did you realise how very wonderful flowers are and how much pleasure they give us? Not only are they beautiful to look at, they smell wonderful and many of them have healing properties.
What do flowers/plants do for us and how do we thank and honour them?
Can you think about how a flower grows?
What does it need?
How can you protect it from the forces which attack it?
What is the role of the various insects you find in your garden, for example ladybirds? worms?, etc.

Get a container of soil from your garden and look very closely at it.
How did it get there?
What is it made of?
How many creatures can you find in this small amount of soil?

Plant a bean in this pot of soil and watch it grow. Take very good care of it. Ask your mum or dad if you can have a small area in your garden or in a window box to plant some flowers, herbs, vegetables, or perhaps a few of each. Look after them very carefully and watch them grow. Perhaps you could also ask mum or dad if a little bit of your garden could be allowed to grow wild, to just 'be', and see what happens. Listen carefully to the garden sounds and perhaps you could compose your own 'Garden Symphony'.

ITA

The beautiful royal Princess Ita was born near Waterford City on the south coast of Ireland. When she was born her parents named her Deirdre, an old and beautiful Celtic name for a beautiful baby. Ita grew into a beautiful and gracious young woman. The young princes of the area vied with each other for the attention of this attractive brown-eyed girl. She was pleasant and friendly with all of them and had a wonderful life, riding the horses on her father's estate, attending parties and doing very much the same as all other young girls at that time. She was very musical – she played the lute and sang beautifully.

Ita spent several hours each day in prayer and solitude. She liked to be out of doors wandering in the mountains and beside the stream, which flowed past the end of her garden. She listened to birds singing and could imitate many of them. She had special devotion to the Trinity – three persons in one God. The number three had great significance for our Celtic ancestors, for this reason, and it also represents the wholeness of body, mind and spirit.

One day while out roaming the countryside, Ita had a vision in which three precious stones were given to her to symbolise the three persons of the Trinity.

Her parents hoped she would marry one of the young princes she had befriended. They liked him and they hoped for grandchildren. Ita was their only child, so they were quite shocked when she told them she planned to become a nun. They loved her very much and even though they were disappointed, they realised that her happiness came first.

An angel visited Ita when she was twenty-one years old and told her to go to the foot of the Sliabh Luachra Mountains and start a convent there. In those days convents were not the same as they are nowadays with set structures and rules. Ita was quite free to set her own rules and to organise her community in the way she thought best.

The king offered Ita a big estate on which to found her convent, but she refused. She wanted something much more simple – a small amount of land where they could grow enough food on which to live. So she took only four acres from the king. There she set up her convent. Other young women joined her; some as nuns, others for an education. Boys also came to her convent for an education. One of these boys was Brendan, later to become one of Ireland's best-known saints.

Ita based her spiritual life on prayer, fasting and the keeping of vigils which meant getting up in the night to pray – many contemplative orders of nuns and monks still do this, for example, the Poor Clares and the Cistercians. She went regularly to a hermitage – a place in the mountains where she could be alone and pray continuously.

Ita's fame spread throughout Ireland and beyond. She became the foster mother of many saints. Her most famous foster child was Brendan. She was much sought after for help and advice. She is said to have written a lullaby for the infant Jesus.

According to Ita there are three things that God especially loves:

1. True faith in God with a pure heart
2. A simple life with a religious spirit
3. Generosity inspired by charity

She also founded many other convents. There are churches and schools named after Ita in Ireland and even in Cornwall, England. Her feast is celebrated on 15 January with prayers and rounds – a set of prayers – at the site of her convent at Killeedy, near Newcastle West, County Limerick. High Mass is celebrated in the local parish church.

Mountains

Have you ever wondered how mountains came into being?
Is there a mountain near where you live?
If so, what is it called?
With a parent or friend, climb this mountain. Make sure you take some water
and some chocolate with you, and wear suitable walking boots and clothing.
How high is your mountain?
What do you notice as you climb?
What is the vegetation like?
Are there things growing there that you have not seen down in the valley?
Which animals make their home on the mountain?
Why do you think this is so?

Is there a stream?
Can you find its source?
Close your eyes and listen to the sound the stream makes.

How does the air change as you go higher up the mountain?
How does the mountain make you feel?
Take a few minutes to admire the colours.
Where is the sun?
Turn to face each of the four directions.
What can you see?
Which direction is the wind coming from?
Why do we sometimes see snow on top of a mountain when it is nice and
sunny in the valley?

Draw a picture of your mountain. Also, make some mountain music.

BRENDAN

This mountaineer and sailor was born on flat, marshy land below the Slieve Mish Mountains on the southern shore of Tralee Bay. He was the son of a small farmer, who fished in Tralee Bay for food. His mother had come from the mountainous area in the Dingle Peninsula. As a young boy, Brendan spent much time cutting turf in the peat bogs near his home. He also went with his father on fishing trips. Soon he learned how to handle a currach and was able to go off fishing with the other young boys who lived close by. He was quite a shy young boy, but popular with his friends because of his helpful, gentle ways.

His parents, who were very religious, encouraged Brendan in his desire to become a monk, so when he was still quite young, he went to a convent run by Ita at Killeedy. There he was educated and became the foster child of Ita. The custom at that time for young boys or girls who wanted to become monks or nuns was to be fostered by a holy woman. I'm sure his parents must have missed him very much. They did have other children, but of course, each is unique and therefore, irreplaceable. When it was time for Brendan to go on to higher studies he went to study with Bishop Erc. From there he went on to the famous monastic school at Clonard. As he wanted to become a priest he went to study with Jarlath – a famous teacher of priests – at Tuam, where Bishop Erc ordained him.

He was a tough and active young man with plenty of energy. He combined his great love of travel with a love of the sea. He travelled around Ireland founding monasteries, the most famous being near his birthplace at Tralee and Clonfert on the river Shannon between Lough Ree and Lough Derg. Young men came from all over Ireland to join these monasteries and they became places of great learning. Young noblemen also came from Europe to be educated by the monks.

In those days, Ireland was referred to as the 'Island of Saints and Scholars'. Brendan loved the mountains and hills of Ireland, but his favourite was Mount Brandon, which is named after him. He went on regular pilgrimages to the top of his mountain. To this day it is an important place of pilgrimage. There is a ruined beehive-shaped oratory at the top (perhaps you could draw one). This mountain is 3,127 feet high and is at the south-western tip of Ireland. One day while Brendan was at the top of Mount Brandon, he looked west and saw a vision of a Blessed Isle in the distance. He immediately planned a trip to this Promised Land. With the help of his monks, he built a currach with a wooden frame, covered with oxhides, tanned with the bark of an oak tree and its joints smeared with fat. When it was ready he set off from Brandon Creek, at the foot of Brandon Mountain. Some believe that he actually reached America.

We are also told of a spiral sea journey Brendan made which lasted for seven years. Two of the people he is said to have visited during this journey are Enda on the Aran Islands and Columcille on Iona.

Brendan lived to a great age and there are many myths and legends about him which show what an extraordinary man he was. We celebrate his feast on 16 May. Many people climb Mount Brandon on that day.

The Sea

Do you know the story of King Canute, who tried to prove to his followers that no one was powerful enough to roll back the sea? Find the story and read it.

Can we roll back the sea?

How much power do we really have?

Do you think it is right to try to control nature?

Look at the sea. Think about its various moods, colours, life-giving qualities, and dangers.

Tim Severin wrote a book, *The Brendan Voyage*, which is a wonderful adventure story. In that book he proves that it was possible for the Celtic

monks of the fourth and fifth centuries to actually reach America in their very simple boats which they called currachs. In Wales they were called coracles.
Find out what the boats were made from. Have you ever seen one?
Do you think you would like to travel all the way to America in one of them?
Find poems and stories which show the power of the sea.
Have you seen the movie *Titanic*?
We need to respect the power of the sea.

Think about creatures that live in the sea. How can we help them?

How do you feel about dumping rubbish in the sea, and the damage done by oil spills? How can we prevent such disasters?

Do you know that 70% of planet Earth is covered by water and that 70% of our bodies are also made up of water? So you can see that we are really connected to our home planet in a very special way. Also, Earth is the only known planet to contain water and thus make life possible for us!

In what ways does the water in the sea differ from that in the river?
Why do you think this is so? Is seawater suitable for drinking? Why not?

Listen to the music of 'The Brendan Voyage' by Liam O'Flynn. You may be able to borrow it from the library or from a friend. Imagine the journey Saint Brendan made from the tip of southern Ireland, through to Newfoundland. Look at an atlas to discover the different places they passed by and the sights they must have seen. Then choose your own favourite part of their journey and paint a picture of it.

NON

Non lived in North Pembrokeshire. She was an attractive girl, tall and slim, with dark flowing hair. She was loved by all who knew her. Many of the local young men wanted to marry her, but she wanted to devote her life to God by becoming a nun. One day, Sant, the King of Cardigan, was riding by and saw her fetching water from the well. He was bowled over by her beauty. He stopped to speak to her.

'Hello, beautiful maiden,' he said. Non replied politely, recognising him as the king. He asked her to accompany him to his castle in the mountains, but she declined, saying, 'Thank you, Sire, but I must return to my home with this water. It is urgently needed by my mother'.

Sant was accustomed to getting his own way, so he was really angry when Non refused to go with him. He jumped off his horse, attacked her, raped her and left her lying injured and crying on the muddy ground beside the well. There she lay until a young shepherd boy, who was returning home with the sheep, found her, helped her up, washed her wounds with the well water, and helped her home.

Soon afterwards, Non realised she was pregnant. The king found out about the baby and wanted it, so Non had to go into hiding. She knew the baby she was carrying was a very special one. Her baby David was born in the midst of a dreadful thunderstorm on the cliffs just south of St David's in Pembrokeshire. A well sprung up at the spot and is still there today. Non fled to Cornwall with her baby and having lived there for some time doing good work among the poor and the sick, she crossed over to Brittany where she spent the rest of her life. Her tomb can still be seen at Finistère.

She is remembered as a gentle and peace-loving person, who also had the gift of healing. We celebrate her feast on 3 March.

Non's Well

This is a picture of Non's Well, said to have sprung up when her son David was born.

The Welsh word for well is 'fynnon'. The Irish word is 'tobar'.
Do you know any place names with these words or the word 'well' in them?

If there is a well near you, visit it, taste the water, feel it on your face. Many wells are said to have healing properties. Sit very quietly beside the well and contemplate the great gift of water.
Could we live without it?
How ought we to care for it?

Think of a way you can give thanks for this blessing. Find some rhymes, poems and stories about wells. Water was sacred to our Celtic ancestors. Find out why.

What do you know about well-dressing ceremonies?
Where did the custom of throwing coins into wells originate?

When you have gathered all this information, perhaps you could organise your own well-dressing ceremony (with the help of a 'not-too-grown-up' adult).

ILLTYD

There is some confusion about the birthplace of this bright young man who went on to become Wales' most famous teacher. Some say he was born near Brecon, a very beautiful part of south Wales. Others claim he was born in Brittany. Certainly, he had connections with Brittany, as he is said to have sailed there with the corn ships to feed the people during a famine. Also, churches and some villages in Brittany bear his name.

A cousin of King Arthur, Illtyd was a privileged young man. He received a good education in France from Bishop Germanus, but had no desire to become a monk. He enjoyed fishing and hunting and spent much of his time in Paris. He became a soldier and returned to Britain to join King Arthur's army. He married a very beautiful young lady called Trynihad. They had a happy life together. We are not sure whether they had any children or not.

One day Illtyd was out hunting with about fifty friends. He wandered off, and while he was gone, all his friends were engulfed in a morass of mud and died. He was so upset by this that he decided to renounce the world. One morning, he went with his wife and some attendants to the banks of a river in South Glamorgan in Wales, and spent the night there in a hut made of reeds.

The next morning he got up and sent his wife and the attendants away and went to the banks of the river and became a hermit, believing he could serve God better alone. He built a church, bathed daily in the cold river water and got up in the middle of the night to pray. Soon he was joined by other men who wanted to live a monastic life. The valley between the River Thaw and the River Ewenny, where he founded his monastery, was very beautiful. The grass was said to be olive green: in spring it was covered with vibrant, yellow gorse; all through summer it was an array of colour; and in autumn it was covered with red and yellow bracken. The monks cultivated the land, lived a simple life and ate only the vegetables they grew and the fish they caught in the river. The monastery was where Llantwit Major now stands. Llan is a Welsh word meaning enclosure where monks lived, or holy place.

Illtyd's fame as a teacher spread. He was the first great teacher of saints in Wales. Soon students flocked to him, the most famous of whom was David, who became the patron of Wales. At one time, Illtyd left his monastery and spent a whole year alone in a cave, praying and fasting.

The King of Glamorgan was out hunting one day with his courtiers and hounds. The fawn they were chasing was terrified and ran into Illtyd's cell for protection. He stayed with Illtyd, who trained him to draw wood, and other light domestic tasks. We celebrate Illtyd's feastday on 6 November. Many boys in Wales are named Illtyd after this famous man.

Rivers

Trace a river to its source.
How does water feel?
Can you see to the bottom?
Are there any creatures living in the stream?

Watch how it flows. Imagine the stream drying up.
What do you think would happen to the creatures that make their home in it?
Could we live without water?

Look at the land bordering a river.
What is it like?
What creatures can you see grazing on this land?
Why were towns built on riverbanks?
Is your town built on a river?
What is it called?
Where does it join the sea?

Close your eyes for a few minutes and think what a blessing water is. Offer thanks for this blessing by creating a dance in praise of the river – your very own 'Riverdance'! You can find some suitable music. If you get some friends to join you, you could create something really special.

Find out about composers who wrote music about water. Find some poems or stories about rivers.

Can you name five of the longest rivers in the world? Do you know where they are? Look at your atlas.

DAVID

David, Non's son, was a quiet, shy boy, very much loved by his mother, being her only child. We don't know a great deal about his early childhood. When he was old enough, he studied with Illtyd at his school at Llantwit Major. He worked hard and got on well. Illtyd was so impressed with David that he sent him to study with a famous teacher called Paulinus, who was blind. One day, David touched Paulinus' eyes and his sight was restored. David always wanted to devote his life to God and eventually he became a priest, and then a bishop. He is reported to have founded twelve monasteries. We do not really know where they all are except one at Glastonbury, another at Bath and of course, the main settlement at St David's (which was not called St David's then).

Lots of young men joined David at his monastery, where they led strict lives. They worked hard in the fields all day. They ate only food they grew themselves, and they drank only water, which may have been the reason David was called the Waterman. They only spoke when it was absolutely necessary! It must have been a really happy place to be.

One night an angel appeared to David and told him to prepare for a journey. The very next day, he set off on a pilgrimage to Jerusalem with two companions. (Can you imagine going on such a long journey by land and sea at such short notice?) It was quite a hazardous journey, but off they went. David was made an archbishop before returning to Wales.

On his return, he continued to live his simple, austere way of life at St David's for many more years, performing miracles, healing and teaching people. After he died, he became the Patron Saint of Wales. His feastday is on 1 March and is celebrated throughout Wales with music and song.

Welsh Emblems

The national emblems of Wales are the daffodil and the leek. Either is worn by Welsh people on St David's Day.

Plant a daffodil bulb.

What makes it grow?
Can you make it grow?

Contemplate the mystery of this tiny bulb growing into a magnificent flower, written about by poets and painted by artists. At the beginning of March carefully pick a bunch of daffodils and give them to somebody you love, or someone who might need cheering up.

Do you know any poems about daffodils?
Find some, and write out your favourite one in your best writing. Decorate and frame it.

The leek is a vegetable for your health and nourishment, said to have been grown by St David in the monastery garden. Plant some leeks in your garden. With the help of a grown-up make some cawl soup (popular in Wales). Cawl is the Welsh word for soup. You'll find the recipe in a cookery book.

Do leeks have a smell?
What do they taste like?

Examine a leek closely. Find out all you can about this important vegetable.
Try to do a detailed drawing of one.

COLUMCILLE

Gartan, County Donegal, set in green fertile land beside a lake to the east of the Derryveagh Mountains, was the birthplace of this lively, athletic young man with royal connections. His father was the great-grandson of Niall of the Nine Hostages who had been High King of Ireland for twenty-seven years. He had been a fierce pirate and is thought to have been responsible for kidnapping Patrick. His mother was the daughter of one of the kings of Leinster. Columcille is said to have been born on a Thursday. He was baptised Columba, but later became known as Columcille. This extraordinary young man had an idyllic childhood. He grew tall and strong among the mountains and hills of this beautiful, rugged country. He was an excellent sportsman and competed against other young men of the county in running, jumping and javelin-throwing. In fact, whatever he chose to do he could do well. But he was not conceited. The other boys liked him very much and he was always included in their activities. He lived most of his life out of doors. Along with his physical skills, he was a brilliant scholar, sang beautifully and wrote poetry.

When he was a teenager he was sent off to school. This was customary in those days. Privileged young men and women were sent to be educated by monks or nuns. Columcille was sent to Moville to become a disciple to Finnian. He worked hard at school and learned much about the love of God. He left Moville as a deacon. Because of his great talent and love of poetry he was sent to study with a bard in Leinster. He enjoyed his time there and spent hours wandering in the Wicklow Mountains writing beautiful poetry. Some of his poetry still survives.

You may be able to find some. Look in one of the old Celtic books in the library.

By this time Columcille had decided to become a monk, so he went on to the monastic school at Clonard, where, coincidentally, his teacher was again called Finnian, known as the tutor of Irish saints. Columcille was one of this distinguished band who later became known as the twelve apostles of Ireland. From Clonard, he went to study with Mobhi at Glasnevin, which is now a suburb of Dublin. He had to leave there quickly because of an outbreak of bubonic plague. Luckily, he had already been ordained a priest before he left and he was one of the few people who escaped the plague. He was still quite a young man when he founded his first monastery – in the middle of an oak grove which had previously been a sacred site to the druids. Columcille had a great love for trees and is said to have built his monastery without cutting down a single tree. This monastery in the oak grove is where the city of Derry stands today. He also founded monasteries at Durrow and Kells. He loved books and spent much time transcribing the gospels and psalter and creating beautiful illuminated manuscripts. He also travelled widely in Ireland. All we know for certain is that in 563 AD he set off in a currach with twelve disciples and on the eve of Pentecost they landed on the small island of Iona on the west coast of Scotland. There they set up a monastery, and there is still a monastic settlement on Iona today which attracts pilgrims from all over the world.

Columcille became involved in the political affairs of Scotland and helped the different communities to live in harmony.

He missed Ireland very much, but he did manage to get back on occasional visits to his monasteries at Derry, Durrow and Kells. Columcille is one of the best known of all the Celtic saints. Although he was strong and energetic, he could be gentle and kind, for he loved people and animals. It is said that he asked God for three things:

- virginity
- wisdom
- the love of pilgrimage

We celebrate his feast on 9 June.

Trees

'I think that I shall never see
a poem lovely as a tree
A tree that may in summer
wear a nest of robins in her hair'.

Can you find this lovely poem by Joyce Kilmer?

Find a tree and make friends with it. Rub your cheek on the bark; put your arms around it; smell it. Is the tree alive?

If you can get a stethoscope, press it firmly against the tree, keeping it still. You may have to try several places before you find the best spot to hear the tree's heartbeat.

Which creatures make their homes in your tree?

Are there any plants living on the tree?

Sit very still and silently under the tree for some time and listen to the sounds. See the roots of the tree burrowing deep into the earth.

Could we live without trees?

Discover their very important role in the web of life. Take a bark rubbing from your tree. Frame it and hang it in a special place. Do some leaf prints on a plain piece of fabric or T-shirt.

Look at your tree in the different seasons; notice how it changes.

At which time of year do you prefer your tree?

When it is resting in winter? Budding in spring? In full bloom in summer? Or in its colourful autumn splendour as it's about to shed its leaves?

Do you know what calligraphy is?

It is the art of beautiful writing. It was an art practised by Columcille as he copied the Gospels and decorated them beautifully. If you've seen the Book of Kells, or a copy of it, you will know what I mean. Write a poem about your special tree in beautiful writing, put a border around it and decorate it. Ask an adult to put it in a frame for you. You can then hang it in a special place as a constant reminder of your own very special tree.

BRYNACH

Brynach was the tall, dark, handsome son of an Irish chieftain. He loved to roam the hills and valleys of County Wicklow on the east coast of Ireland. He fished in the lakes, climbed the mountains and sailed along the coast in his currach.

He abandoned his position and all his wealth and set off on a pilgrimage to Rome. While he was there he heard about Jesus and decided he would like to become a follower. In a dream an angel told him about David in west Wales. So he decided to visit him. When he arrived at Milford Haven in west Wales, he was overawed by the splendour and beauty of the coastline as he sailed up the waterway.

As soon as the local chieftain's daughter saw Brynach she fell in love with him. He didn't want anything to do with her because he had made his mind up to become a monk and devote his life to God. She was really upset and angered by Brynach's rejection of her and sent a group of her father's warriors to attack Brynach. One of the men stabbed him with a spear. He managed to escape but he was bleeding badly. He went and washed in a well that has since become known as Ffynnon Goch and immediately the wound healed over.

Brynach continued north to the Gwaun Valley to escape his attackers. He built a church at Pontifan in the heart of a magical wood dating back to the Ice Age. Next he travelled along the river Nevern. An angel told him to keep going until he saw a sow and her piglets on a riverbank. Here he built another church. He spent many years living as a hermit in the Nevern area, dressed in animal skins and following a vegetarian diet. He spent long periods in solitude in Ty Canol woods and many days and nights at the top of Carn Ingli – the hill of the angels – communing with the angels. People say that on a clear day he could see the Wicklow hills from here, so perhaps that is why he spent so much time at the top!

We celebrate his feast in Wales on 7 April. He is remembered with great affection, particularly in north Pembrokeshire.

Angels

Do you believe in angels?

I do. My angel is tall and slim with long golden hair. Her name is Clarity. Close your eyes and 'see' your angel. Get to know her/him.

What does she/he look like?

Talk to your angel. Ask for help and advice. Draw a picture or make a clay model of your own special angel and keep her/him close to you to remind you that you are never alone.

GOBNAIT

The Aran Islands are situated off the west coast of Ireland. They are islands of spectacular beauty. A long time ago, before people knew the world was round, they thought these islands were the end of the world. Gobnait lived on the most beautiful of these islands called Inis Thiar, which, in English, means 'the western isle'.

Her dad fished for their food and they also had some sheep and goats, which grazed along the high crags. When she was not helping her father in his currach, Gobnait enjoyed climbing along the rugged cliffs.

One day while Gobnait was skipping along the beach an angel appeared to her and told her to go to a place where she would find nine white deer grazing. She was very sad to leave her parents but she knew that she must obey the angel.

Her mother prepared some food for her and her father took her to the mainland in his currach. She kissed him goodbye and set off on her travels through southern Ireland. She founded convents along the way, one at Kilgobnet (Gobnait's church) in County Waterford and one at Clondrohid in County Cork where she saw three deer grazing. Next she crossed to Ballymakeera where she saw six deer. As she crossed the river and climbed up a grassy bank she saw nine deer lazily enjoying the fresh grass on this pleasant slope. There was a freshwater spring in a little grove of lime trees and plots of good land among the rocks.

Here she stayed and built her convent. Many of the local girls joined her and soon they had a thriving community who did a lot of good work in the area around Ballyvourney.

Gobnait was a good and dedicated nurse and by her special care of the sick she kept the plague out of Ballyvourney when it was raging through the rest

of Ireland. She is still remembered in this lovely mountainous district. Her feastday on 11 February is celebrated with a pilgrimage to her shrine. She is also remembered as a beekeeper.

Bees

Bees play a very important role in the web of life.

What do you know about them?

They make honey and wax, but they are much more valuable as pollenators. Some bees are solitary creatures while others are quite sociable. They dance and sing, perfectly secure in their place in the Universe.

Before we had sugar, honey was used as a sweetener. Have you tasted honey from the honeycomb?

Follow a bee to a flower. You must keep very quiet and still. Wonder at the intelligence and industry of this fragile creature.

Find out all you can about bees. You will be amazed at the contribution they make to your delight and well-being. In return for their gift, perhaps you can make sure their environment is safe. Let us return blessing for blessing.

WINEFRIDE

This demure and beautiful girl was the only daughter of a rich and brave soldier who lived in the north-east of Wales. She was niece to a famous Welsh saint called Bueno. She was a studious girl with a love of animals and birds. Her uncle taught her to read and write and told her Bible stories. She loved to sit at his feet and learn. Soon she decided that she wanted to give her life to God as a nun. She spent a great deal of time with Bueno learning about religious life.

One of the local chieftains liked Winefride. He had wanted her to be his wife but she refused to be his wife. He was accustomed to having what he wanted so Winefride's refusal hurt him deeply. He was so angry that one day he chased her with his sword. She ran to the church, but he hit out at her and cut her head off. Luckily Bueno was in the church at the time and he put her head back on. A well sprung up at the place where she fell, and the ground opened up and swallowed the young chieftain.

Wineride's father gave her land in a remote mountain valley on which to build a convent. Together with several other pious, young girls, she received the veil from Bueno. Winefride is said to have been a very good seamstress. She made the habits for her nuns and also a new habit for Bueno each year. She worked among the poor and the sick in and around Holywell, where her convent was. She and her community were renowned for their simple way of life and their care for birds and animals. When her Uncle Bueno died, Winefride moved to Denbighshire where she became abbess of a convent. The title 'Friend of Peace' has been given to her because she continuously promoted peace and harmony among all whom she came in contact.

The well which sprung up at the beheading of Winefride is the most copious natural spring in all of Britain. It is free from organic matter and has a beautiful smell. It is an important place of pilgrimage today and its healing waters have cured several people. Many ancient churches are dedicated to Winefride and we celebrate her feast on 3 November.

Celtic Blessing

Deep peace of the running wave to you
Deep peace of the silent stars
Deep peace of the flowing air to you
Deep peace of the quiet earth
May peace, may peace
May peace fill your soul
Let peace, let peace
Let peace make you whole

Do you know other Celtic Blessings?

Try to find some.

Pilgrimage

A pilgrimage is a journey, a special kind of journey taken by pilgrims who travel to holy places. A pilgrimage is a spriritual journey. Think about journeys you have made.

Have you travelled on land, water or in the air?
Why did you make your journey?
Who accompanied you?
Did you enjoy the journey or were you more concerned with the arrival (that is, the place you were travelling to or whom you were going to see when you got there)?

The people you've been reading about in this book made pilgrimages to sacred places to pray and to think about those who had gone there a long time ago. Some people go on pilgrimages to be cured from an illness; to offer thanks; or to ask for some favour.
Do you know of anybody who has gone on a pilgrimage to Lourdes or to Knock or to Lough Derg?

People go on pilgrimages to holy wells – wells that are connected with particular saints because of particular cures the well is reputed to have. Different wells have different healing properties.

Our life story is a journey that has occurred over billions of years, that we have travelled to be where we are now. Close your eyes and think of your own amazing journey – from your enormous burst of explosive energy, through molten, bubbling rock, turgid, sizzling, cooling seas, when you stood upright as a plant, ambled as a dinosaur, flew as a bird, swam as a fish, right through to your present state. You are as old as the universe and as young as a newborn baby. What a wonder you are!

Paint a picture showing your spectacular evolution.